MY DOG

How to Have a Happy, Healthy Pet

NORTHWORD

First published in the U.S.A. in 2001 by
NorthWord Press
5900 Green Oak Drive
Minnetonka, MN 55343
1-800-328-3895

ISBN 1-55971-793-9

This edition edited by Barbara K. Harold

A catalog record for this book is available from the
Library of Congress, Washington, DC.

Color reproduction by Sang Choy, Singapore
Printed by Kyodo Printing Co. (S'pore) Pte Ltd
Printed in Singapore

10 9 8 7 6 5 4 3 2 1

Conceived and produced by Weldon Owen Pty Limited
59 Victoria Street, McMahons Point, NSW, 2060, Australia
A member of the Weldon Owen Group of Companies
Sydney • San Francisco • London

Weldon Owen Pty Ltd
Publisher: Sheena Coupe
Associate Publisher: Lynn Humphries
Senior Designer: Kylie Mulquin
Editorial Coordinator: Tracey Gibson
Editorial Assistant: Marney Richardson
Production Manager: Helen Creeke
Production Coordinator: Kylie Lawson
Vice President International Sales: Stuart Laurence

Project Editor and Text: Lynn Cole
Consultant: Paul McGreevy, B.V.Sc., Ph.D., M.R.C.V.S.
Illustrator: Janet Jones
Commissioned Photography: Stuart Bowey, Ad-Libitum

Credits and Acknowledgments

[t=top, b=bottom, l=left, r=right]

All photographs by **Stuart Bowey, Ad-Libitum** except: **Corbis Images** 1c, 4b, 21tl, 22l, 28t, 34c, 44r, 45tl; **PhotoDisc** 7l, 7br, 8bl, 11tr, 12tr, 16l, 26t, 34t, 35t, 40t; **Tony Stone Images** 12l, 32tl, 32b.

Weldon Owen would like to thank the following people for their assistance in the preparation of this book: Lorraine Abercrombie and "Tess";
Sarah Anderson; Leigh Audette and "Boss"; Helen Bateman and "Bonnie"; Esther Blank and "Max"; Eliza Bowey; Jess Bowey; Jenni Bruce and "Stella";
Michelle Burk and "Jacko"; Matina Butcher and "Tuffy," "Sparky," "Justine," and "Jackie"; Penny Cass and "Wilma"; Lynn Cole and "Abel"; Dorothy Cooper
and "June"; Lindy Coote and "Boo"; Donna and Tom Devitt and "Kinka"; Julia Edworthy and "Bingo"; Ann and Andrew Finlaison and "Blake"; Kevan and
Verena Gardner and "Floyd"; Felicity Gates and "Tom"; Matt Gavin-Wear and "Amber"; Margaret Giles and "Jessica"; Kathy Gorman and "Carlo";
Peta Gorman; Gwynneth Grant and "Max"; Kerri Hancock and "Marley"; Michael Hann; Robin Hill and "Red" and "Black"; Emilia Kahrimanis and "Lulabelle";
Mary-Lou Keating and "Clair"; Suzie Kennedy and "Eddie"; Jane Lamb; Gordon and Sue Lasslett and "Madison"; Lubasha Macdonald and "Tigra";
Rosemary Marin-Guzman and "Biggles"; Max and Glenda Mason and "Taaris"; Andrew McIntyre and "Daisy"; Margaret and Kris Papadatos and "Rosie"
and "Faith"; Dan Penny and "Jaffa"; Kevin Peters and "Kossie"; Vicki Pocklington and "Tyler"; Alan Poulton and "Missy," "Larsen," and "Thelma"; Angela
Price and "Bramble"; Jacqueline Richards and Winona Wiles and "Skipper"; Peter and Lydia Sparkowoski and "Teddy"; P. and G.J. Wakefield and "Thomas";
Nola Westren and "Amber"; Ivan and Ellis Zalac and "Jack" and "Culo".

MY DOG

How to Have a Happy, Healthy Pet

NORTHWORD PRESS
Minnetonka, Minnesota

Contents

Which dog is best for your home and family?

On the following pages you will meet just a few of the most popular dog breeds, but there are many other dogs, of all sizes, to choose from. This book will help you get off to a good start with your new pet. While you help it to understand and obey the rules in your house, you will be making a very special friend for life!

Being a good owner

When you and your family decide to have a dog, think carefully about why you want it and what you want to do with it. You must have a safe place for it to live and be prepared to spend quite a lot of time taking it for walks every day, training, and looking after it. (There are also less pleasant jobs, such as using a pooper-scooper. And some breeds, such as Basset Hounds, make messes by drooling a lot.) Your new dog will be part of your family for a long time to come. Breeds such as this Maltese-Bichon Frise mix can live for up to 16 years.

Puppy or adult?

Puppies are like babies—they learn what is safe and what is not safe by making mistakes. And you must not get angry with them. While they are learning, they must be kept out of danger. Perhaps an older dog that has already had some training would be better for you.

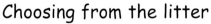

You might need help from a grown-up to handle a big dog like this Boxer, but all adult dogs can be obedient if they are properly trained

Puppies, like this Rhodesian Ridgeback, enjoy all kinds of fun and must be gently taught what they are and are not allowed to do in the house

Choosing from the litter

Both males and females make excellent pets, so it's your family's choice. Confident, outgoing animals, like these Australian Shepherd puppies, are often easier to train, because they are willing to try out new things. Timid, nervous dogs may sometimes bite because they are frightened.

Purebred...

These dogs may be expensive, because they have been raised in a special way. But they make great pets.

Golden Retriever

Size Medium to large
Personality Playful, loving and loyal. Loves to play fetch
Place to live Needs a yard, but likes to be allowed indoors with the family
Exercise Two big walks or play sessions every day
Feeding Once or twice a day, but don't let it get fat
Grooming Brush and comb two or three times a week

Miniature Poodle

Size Small to medium
Personality Smart, friendly, and loyal. Easy to train
Place to live These dogs are a popular choice for families living in apartments
Exercise Two big walks or play sessions every day
Feeding Two small meals a day
Grooming Brush and comb every day, plus regular clipping by a professional groomer

Standard Poodle

Size Medium to large
Personality Very intelligent and easy to train. Loving and loyal
Place to live Doesn't mind living indoors as long as it gets enough outdoor exercise
Exercise Two big walks or play sessions every day
Feeding Once or twice a day
Grooming Brush and comb every day, plus regular clipping by a professional groomer

Toy Poodle

Size Small
Personality Lively, friendly, and very affectionate. Easy to train and noted for its smartness
Place to live Good choice if you live in an apartment
Exercise Two big walks or play sessions every day
Feeding Two small meals a day
Grooming Brush and comb every day, plus regular clipping by a professional groomer

Dachshund, Smooth (left) and Wirehaired (right)

Size Small or medium

Personality Smart, but can be stubborn

Place to live Adapts well to living in an apartment, but don't let Dachshunds get bored or fat

Exercise Two big walks or play sessions every day

Feeding Twice a day

Grooming Brush short coats once a week and long- and wire-haired coats more often

Size Large (you'll need a grown-up to help handle this dog)

Personality Smart and loyal

Place to live Needs a large yard to play and run

Exercise Needs obedience training and lots of exercise

Feeding Two meals a day, but don't let Rottweilers get fat

Grooming Brush every day with a firm bristle brush or use a hound glove

Rottweiler

Dachshund, Longhaired

Size Large (you'll need an adult to help handle this dog)

Personality Brave and loyal

Place to live Needs a large yard to play and run

Exercise A lot of exercise needed, two big walks a day

Feeding Two meals a day; don't let Boxers get fat

Grooming Brush every day with a firm bristle brush and wipe over with a damp cloth

Size Small

Personality Playful and lively, but can get bossy. Handle gently

Place to live Adapts well to living in an apartment, but likes lots of playing and activity

Exercise Two walks a day—attach the lead to a body harness

Feeding Two small meals a day

Grooming Brush long-haired coats gently every day and short-haired coats twice a week

Boxer

Chihuahua

Size Medium to large
Personality Reliable, very loving, and loyal
Place to live Will adapt to any size of yard, but needs plenty of activity
Exercise Two big walks a day and lots of playing and fun
Feeding Twice a day while a puppy, then once a day
Grooming Brush and comb two or three times a week

Labrador Retriever

Size Medium
Personality Even-tempered
Place to live Doesn't mind if the yard is small as long as it has lots of activity
Exercise Needs plenty of exercise, two big walks a day—can be hard to handle off the leash
Feeding Two small meals a day, but less if it starts to get fat
Grooming Brush regularly with a firm bristle brush

Beagle

Size Small
Personality Brave, lively, loving, and loyal
Place to live A good choice if you live in an apartment
Exercise Likes to run and play; two walks a day
Feeding Two small meals a day; don't give too much meat
Grooming Brush and comb every day—coat can be clipped quite short if you like

Yorkshire Terrier

Size Large (you'll need a grown-up to help handle this dog)
Personality Smart and dependable, loving and loyal. These dogs are easy to train
Place to live Needs a large yard to play and run
Exercise A lot of exercise needed, two big walks a day
Feeding Two or three small meals a day rather than one large
Grooming Brush regularly

German Shepherd

...or mixed breed

Dogs of mixed breed cost far less than purebreds and usually have fewer health problems. They are just as loyal and lovable as any other dog, and always have great personalities.

Unknown mix

Maltese and Chihuahua mix

Bull Terrier mix

Smooth Collie mix

Old English Sheepdog and Border Collie mix

Where to get a dog or puppy

Good breeders want you to have a nice-tempered, healthy dog that will become a loved member of your family. They have known the puppies they breed since birth, but more important, they know the mother. Many animal shelters have well-trained staff who can also help you to choose well. People looking for new homes for purebred dogs often put notices on breed-rescue sites on the Internet.

Puppies may also be found through friends, or advertised in newspapers

Animal shelters

Dogs are found in animal shelters for lots of different reasons. You may have to make more than one trip before you find the dog that is perfect for you, but shelters are good places to find a mixed-breed dog like this cute Beagle mix.

Checking for a healthy puppy

The puppy you choose should be bright-eyed, confident, and alert. This Norwegian Elkhound looks perfect, but it's a good idea to have any new dog checked over by your own vet within a few days of bringing it home.

Ears should be clean and not smelly

Eyes should be bright and not watery

The coat should be glossy and clean

Nose should be moist, cool, and not runny

Mouth should have pink gums, and the breath should smell clean

The puppy should move freely on all four paws

The breeder

Puppies from good breeders, like these Saint Bernards, are already used to being handled by people when the time comes for them to be sold.
Once you have decided on the breed you want, find a breeder that people you know say is reliable. Always ask to see your puppy's mother and, if possible, its father.

Paperwork

When you buy your new pet, the breeder should give you all the puppy's papers, fully completed. These include:

- Pedigree papers
- Certificates for all vaccinations
- A record of its microchip number and the form for providing your address
- Written advice on worming and on any other vaccinations your pet needs
- A diet sheet showing what type of food the puppy is used to and offering some advice on its future diet. (Some breeders will even give you some of the food your puppy has been eating.)

Non-slip
metal bowls

Ceramic
bowl

What to buy before your dog comes home

Looking after your new friend will be easier if you have the right equipment. And shopping for your dog can be fun! You will find lots of choices in pet stores. And your dog will be happy that you are well-prepared for it to join your family.

Bean bag

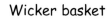

Wicker basket

Puppy playpen

Many people choose an indoor kennel or crate that can be put in a room where there's plenty of activity, say the kitchen, but which can also fit in the car for traveling. This should be a safe place where a dog, like this Staffordshire Bull Terrier puppy, can rest. Your dog may also eat and play there. Never put your pet in the crate as a punishment.

Beds and bowls

Your new pet needs a cozy, comfortable place to sleep. Be sure your dog will be warm enough. It also needs its own food and water bowls. Ceramic or metal bowls are easier to keep clean than plastic bowls. They are also less likely to slip or tip over.

Plush toy

Tug toy

Ball on
a rope

Squeeze
toys

Nylon rope
toy

Rubber ball

Toys

It's better to start with just a few toys, then add a new one when your dog loses interest in the old ones. If you put some away for a while, they will seem new when your dog sees them again. Leave safe chew toys or squeaky balls in your dog's kennel or crate so it won't be bored.

Leather
collar

Nylon
clip
collar

Nylon and
leather
collar

Collars and leashes

Even if your dog has a microchip for identification, it should also wear a tag on its collar with your address or phone number. The Halti collar is good for walking your dog. It lets you guide your pet's head around to the direction you want to go without hurting the dog. Flat collars are best for puppies because they can be adjusted easily as the young dog grows. Be sure the leash is short enough to give you good control of your dog.

Nylon leash

Nylon and
leather
leash

Retractable
leash

A Rhodesian Ridgeback
mix wearing a Halti collar

15

Bringing your new dog home

You want your new dog to settle in happily, so don't be in a rush. Let the new dog introduce itself to family members. Each person can kneel down and let the dog sniff their hand. If it wags its tail and seems friendly, it's okay to pet it or scratch it on the chest and under its chin.

A safe trip
For the trip home, and until your dog learns how to travel in a car, you can put it in a carrier box. This will keep your dog out of harm's way.

Checking out the new place
Let your dog explore its new surroundings at its own pace. But be sure to watch so that it doesn't get into trouble!

Dog-proofing your home
Your home should be as safe as if a small child were coming to stay. People pills and medicines should be stored properly. Kitchen and bathroom cleansers should be out of reach or locked away. Poisonous things used in the garden should also be in a safe place. And don't forget things in the garage, such as antifreeze—they belong well out of the way on a high shelf. You and your parents should make a thorough check inside and outside for hazards like these before your dog comes home.

Meeting your cat

Hold your new dog tightly, **not** the cat.
The cat will probably fluff itself up, hiss, spit,
and run away. Don't let the dog chase the cat.
Then, try to get the dog's attention away from the cat.
You could shake a noisy toy. Repeat the meetings
until the two get used to each other.

Meeting the family

Let the dog choose who it wants to say hello to.
This Whippet-Staffordshire Bull Terrier mix is getting
a gentle welcome. Speak in soft voices and don't
make too much fuss. Small children shouldn't pick
up the dog until they know how to do it properly.

Meeting your other dog

It's best if the two dogs meet in a place neither
dog thinks is theirs, say at the park, as these
mixed breeds are doing. At home, when the
two dogs are together, always give the resident
dog lots of attention so it won't be jealous. You
can also put the new dog in its indoor kennel
or crate until the two start to make friends.

 It's a good idea...

...for you and your new dog
to go to obedience classes.
Your dog will learn that
you are now its leader,
and you must learn to be
a kind leader.

House-training your dog

New dogs need to learn the rules of your home, such as which things they can chew and which they can't. And puppies must be taught to do their business outside. Learning these new things should be fun for your dog! The words used as commands in this book are only suggestions. It doesn't matter what word you choose just as long as everyone uses the same word and applies the same rules.

"Kong" toys

You can stuff these toys with things that smell delicious, such as peanut butter. This Staffordshire Bull Terrier is enjoying getting the food treat out of its hollow rubber toy.

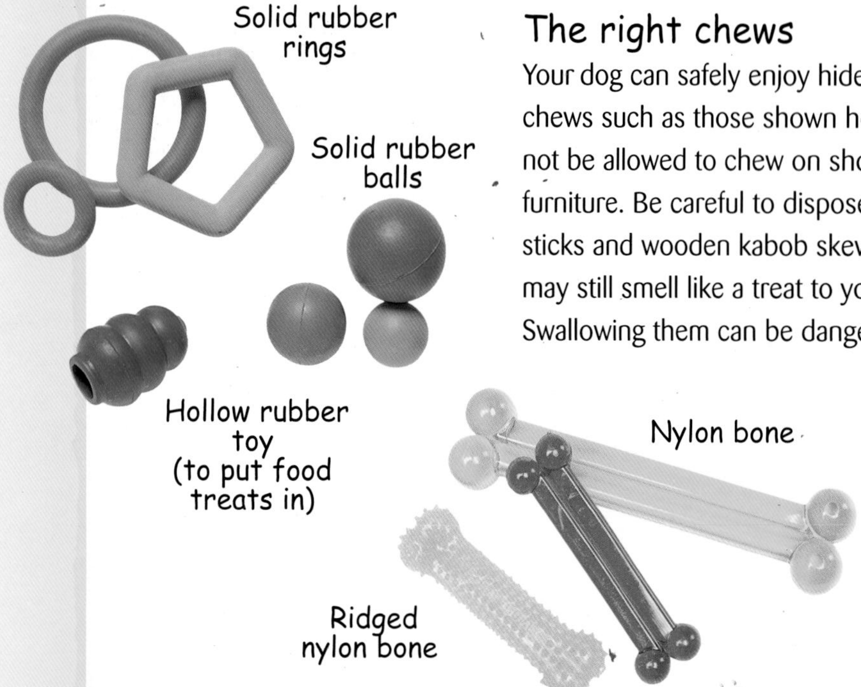

Solid rubber rings

Solid rubber balls

The right chews

Your dog can safely enjoy hide or rubber chews such as those shown here. It should not be allowed to chew on shoes and furniture. Be careful to dispose of Popsicle sticks and wooden kabob skewers, which may still smell like a treat to your dog. Swallowing them can be dangerous.

Hollow rubber toy
(to put food treats in)

Nylon bone

Ridged nylon bone

Dog-proofing your yard

Dogs find out about things by smelling and tasting. That's fine if it's something that can be eaten, but some things aren't meant to be chewed—power cables, for example. Dogs are also pretty good at finding holes in and under fences, so it's important that a grown-up checks your yard carefully. Make sure the gate closes properly, too.

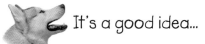 It's a good idea...

...from the very start, to always use the same words when you ask your dog to do something. Speak in a happy but firm voice.

Toilet training

Take your puppy or dog out in the yard from time to time during the day (quite often for a young puppy). You should do it right after your dog eats, first thing in the morning, and last thing at night. Be patient and wait until it starts to do its business, then praise it quietly. Don't take the dog inside until it has finished. This Maltese is asking to be taken outside.

When "accidents" happen

Your dog is sure to have an occasional "accident." Don't make a fuss. Just clean up the mess and rinse the place thoroughly so that no smell remains. (If the smell is still there, your dog might be tempted to go to the toilet there again.)

Empty the mouth

You can train your dog to give up what is in its mouth by offering something it wants more, such as a treat. When it drops the object, say "Drop," and praise it. Don't make it a tug-of-war, or it will think you want to play that game. When the dog has the idea, gradually get it used to giving up bones in the same way.

Feeding your dog

Canned food

Semi-moist food

Dry food

Nearly all dogs like to taste new and different foods. They may even try to beg from your dinner table. Keep your dog away from the table while people are eating—if you feed it tidbits from the table, you are teaching it to be a pest! It's best to feed your dog from its own bowl after the family has eaten. This will help it be polite around mealtimes!

The right amount
Read the label to see how much food to give. For young dogs, divide the food into two or more meals and do not give it all at once. Some older dogs, such as this Border Collie, eat just one meal a day. Always provide plenty of fresh, clean drinking water.

Kinds of food
The type of food you give your dog is up to you. But remember that a sudden change of food sometimes causes diarrhea. To change foods, mix a small amount of the new food with the old. Add a little more at each meal until it is getting all new food.

Giving a treat

You can train your pet to take a food treat gently from your hand, as this Labrador is doing. Try to keep your hand very still when offering the treat—don't get scared and pull your hand away or your dog will learn to snatch at treats with its teeth. If you stay calm, your dog will soon get the right idea.

Stealing the trash

Although garbage smells bad to us, dogs want to explore the smells. It doesn't mean that your dog is hungry. This Australian Shepherd is doing it even though it's already been fed. Just be sure to put the trash where your dog can't get at it.

Dangers with food

Some foods that people enjoy are really bad for dogs—which doesn't mean that they won't eat them if they get the chance. Chocolate is dangerous for all dogs, and even a small piece can kill a little dog. Other things to keep well out of reach are cooked bones, the strings and stretchy bags used to hold roasts together, kabob skewers, and, strangely enough, onions. Large amounts of fat can also make your dog very sick.

Exercising your dog

Playing together is a great way to become close friends with your pet, and the wonderful thing about dogs is that they're always ready and willing to play—they're never too busy. Remember to play outside games when it's not too hot and stop before your dog is really tired, especially while it's still a puppy.

The backyard

If you have a good-sized backyard, your dog will find ways to play alone. A special dog flap in the door is a great idea—this American Bulldog can go in and out whenever it pleases.

Regular exercise

You should take your dog for at least a half-hour walk every day, like this mixed breed's owner is doing. Playing games with your dog is another way to keep it healthy and stop it from getting fat. This will keep your dog from being bored, too. (A walk is also good for you!)

A game of fetch the ball

Many dogs, like this Smooth Collie mix, love to chase and retrieve a ball that you throw, and this is very good exercise. Encourage your dog to bring the ball back and give it to you by offering a treat. Never chase the dog to take the ball, or get into a tug-of-war if you don't want that to become part of the game.

Swimming

Dogs don't have to be taught how to swim—they can just do it. Some dogs, like this Australian Cattle dog, love it, but only let them swim where your parents say it is safe.

 It's a good idea...

...to make sure your dog has plenty of fun, activities, and exercise. A bored dog is more likely to get into mischief than a busy one.

Agility games

Some people enjoy training dogs such as this Golden Retriever to compete against others in contests called agility trials. They jump, climb, and run through tunnels.

If this sounds like fun, you can set up some low jumps or other obstacles and see if you both like this kind of game. Be sure to wait until your dog is at least one year old—puppies can hurt themselves jumping.

150 mm
200 mm
250 mm

Grooming your dog

Grooming keeps your dog's coat clean and shiny. Also, it's a very good way to get your dog used to having every part of its body touched. If you start when it's a puppy, handling even its ears and toes very gently, your dog will be calm when visiting the vet or a professional groomer.

Special attention

- Your dog's teeth need to be cleaned once a year by your vet. You can also help by rubbing them regularly with a piece of a soft towel over your finger. Use a dab of special dog toothpaste that is safe for your dog to swallow.
- Trim any long hairs between the toes or pads with scissors. You may need help with this.
- Ask a professional groomer or a vet to clip your dog's nails.

Bathing your dog

Unless they have rolled in something smelly, most dogs only need a bath once or twice a year. Brushing spreads the natural oils and cleans the coat much better than soap and water.

1. Try to give a bath on a warm day and start early. Thick coats, especially, take a long time to dry. First, brush the coat well to get rid of tangles—when a tangle gets wet it tightens up and is even harder to get rid of. If possible, wash with warm water.
2. Use a shampoo made for dogs or babies, and keep suds and water away from your dog's eyes and ears. Bathing this Golden Retriever is made easier by having someone help to hold it still.
3. Rinse well. Stand back when your dog shakes itself!
4. Use towels to dry the coat as much as possible. Let your dog run around to warm up. Brush its coat again to dry it quickly.

Using a pin-cushion brush

These brushes are good for short, curly coats (like Poodles have) that are likely to become matted. The best way to avoid this is to brush your pet every day, paying special attention to tangles when they are just starting. (Poodles hardly shed any hair at all.)

Using a slicker brush

These are good for removing loose hairs from short, thick coats (like a Labrador's). Brush your dog's coat mainly in the direction it grows. If you run into a tangle, loosen it gently with your fingers before continuing with the grooming.

Using a wide-toothed comb

Use these combs on long, soft coats (like a Collie's) and for combing through tangles in all coats, after loosening them with your fingers. Be careful not to push the teeth of the comb into your pet's skin.

Playing with your dog

The more you play with your dog, the better you will get to know each other. Your dog also needs to play rough-and-tumble games with other dogs. This helps it use up its spare energy and learn about being a dog. Most dogs are friendly, but when you play with them always be careful not to hurt them by accident in case they bite.

Sleep time

Young puppies love to play but, like human babies, they need a lot of sleep. Just wait until it wakes up again and it will be ready for more fun.

It's a good idea...

...to play ball games only where your dog can't run out onto a road.

Picking your dog up

A puppy (like this Toy Poodle) must feel safe when you pick it up or it will struggle to get away. Hold it firmly with one arm around its chest under its front legs. The other arm should be under its back legs. It won't like being grabbed around the belly and having both ends dangling.

26

Safe games

When your dog gets very excited it may forget its manners and jump up at you or knock you over. If this starts to happen, stop the game and play a quieter one until it calms down again. Always put away any toys, such as balls, at the end of the game—so your dog remembers that you are the leader.

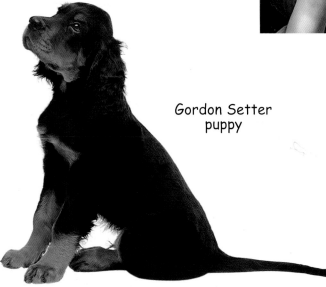

Gordon Setter puppy

Sensitive parts

A dog's tail is part of its backbone. Never pull the tail or grab it during a chasing game, because you might hurt or seriously injure the dog. Always handle the head and ears gently, too, and never pull the ears.

Toys and games

Different breeds of dogs often like different kinds of games. For example, terriers will pounce on the ball and try to shake it, while Labradors will turn every game into a tug-of-war. This Miniature Schnauzer is trying to get at the food treats inside its ball. You will soon find out which kind of game is your dog's favorite!

Traveling with your dog

A good way to get your pet used to car travel is to take it with you on lots of short drives before you take it on a long trip. Going to the park is perfect, because your dog will be looking forward to playing there. Don't feed it just before you leave in case it gets carsick, but always take water if you will be away from home for long.

Camping
Many campsites allow dogs, but your pet may have to be tied up for safety reasons. Be sure to take a supply of the food it is used to—you may not be able to buy it later.

When your dog can't go with you

The best thing is for a friend of the family to stay in your house to look after your pet. If that's not possible you may have to choose a boarding kennel. Ask other dog owners if they know a good kennel and visit it before leaving your pet there. Make sure your dog's vaccinations are up to date.

Safe inside

Even though dogs love to put their heads out the car window and feel the wind in their faces, it's best if they keep their heads inside. Nasty things can get blown into their eyes. You must never leave your pet locked in a hot car—if it gets too hot your dog can quickly become "dehydrated," which means that there isn't enough water in its body.

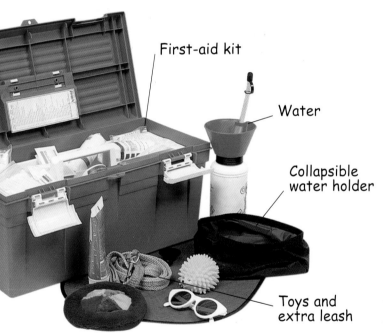

First-aid kit

Water

Collapsible water holder

Toys and extra leash

Accessories

Your first-aid kit should include a booklet showing what to do for your dog in an emergency. And don't forget a pooper-scooper or plenty of plastic bags for clean-ups.

Back seat safety

In the picture above, netting stops this German Shepherd mix from getting into the front seat with the driver. Below, the dog is wearing a body harness clipped onto a seatbelt.

Regular health checks

Your dog can't tell you when it feels sick, so you must try to be a good detective and notice all the little clues and signs that show there's a problem. Every time you groom your pet, notice anything that's different. Giving your dog these little check-ups will help it to stay healthy.

Checking your dog's paws and nails

This young Cocker Spaniel is having its paws checked for grass seeds, grit, or gravel that can get stuck between the pads. If you notice your pet is limping, gently check its paws and carefully remove whatever is hurting. You may need help from an adult to do this if the foot is very sore. If the nails are very long, they can be clipped by the vet or a professional groomer.

Checking eyes and ears

Your pet's eyes should look bright and clear, with no redness or pus. If the dog is squinting, take it to the vet—there could be something in the eye. The inside of your dog's ears should be dry and look clean and pink. If your dog is shaking its head or scratching at its ears, or the ears are smelly, sore, or swollen, take it to the vet.

Checking for fleas and ticks

If you see your dog scratching a lot, it may be because it has fleas. (Look for black flea dirt on the skin—because this is partly blood, it will turn red if you wet it on a piece of tissue.) Ticks climb aboard when dogs sniff about in bushes, so they most often bite on the dog's head and neck. The best way to find them is to run your fingers carefully over every bit of your dog's skin, feeling for tiny lumps. Be sure to look under the collar and in the ears. Your vet will tell you what to do about these pests.

Flea

Tick

Vaccination

Injecting a vaccine into an animal is a way of protecting it from diseases it might catch from other animals. Your vet will tell you what vaccinations your dog needs and when it should have them. Then it's up to you to see that your dog gets them. If you don't, your dog could become very ill. You could get a small calendar and make a note on it when each shot is due.

Visiting the vet

Like people, all pets get sick from time to time. Usually it's nothing serious, but just as you sometimes have to see the doctor, your dog sometimes needs some help to get well again. Your dog should also have an annual check-up when it's not sick, so that the vet can be sure your dog is healthy.

Be prepared

Some dogs are frightened when they are put on the examination table. You can help your dog stay calm by practicing at home ahead of time. Be extra careful that your dog doesn't fall off. Each time you practice, your dog can get used to standing on the table for a little longer.

Quiet time

This Collie puppy is sick and needs to stay quiet. Its owner is spending some time with it, talking softly and stroking it gently in places that are not sore. This will help the puppy feel less sad and lonely. Don't let too many visitors at a time near your sick dog.

When your pet is sick

One of the first things the vet will do is take your dog's temperature. If this is high, it means that your dog may have an infection. Your dog won't feel hungry while it's ill, but it's very important that it drinks some water. If not, it can quickly become dehydrated. Having too little water in its body can be a serious problem for your dog. If it has diarrhea or is vomiting, it can become dehydrated very quickly.

Tell-tale signs

If your dog seems suddenly to be losing weight or putting it on and you haven't changed its food, see your vet. If you notice any of the signs below (**the ones in bold type like this are URGENT**), and the problem goes on for more than a day, see your vet.

- If your dog **seems very sleepy**, or doesn't want to play, or is limping, or is **having trouble standing up**
- If it is not interested in food
- If its breath smells awful
- If any part of the body seems sore, or tender, or swollen
- If it is **straining when it tries to go to the toilet**, or it has diarrhea (urgent if **the poo looks bloody**)
- If it vomits more than twice (urgent if **vomit is bloody or dark**)
- If it **can't urinate**, or is going more or less often than usual

- If it seems to be thirsty all the time and is always lapping at puddles when you go for a walk
- If it is drooling more than usual
- If it is coughing, or **breathing in a strange way**, or **sneezing a lot**
- If it is **squinting**, or there is goo coming from the eyes, or the eyes are red
- If it keeps on scratching, especially at its ears, or shaking its head, or the ears are smelly, or there is goo coming from them
- If it is **pawing at its mouth** (there may be something stuck there)
- If it has a sore that won't heal

Having puppies

If your dog has a litter of puppies, your home will be jam-packed full of fun! When they are first born, the puppies will stay close to their mother. No matter how much you want to pick them up and show them to all your friends, you must not. When the mother is ready to "share" them with people, she'll let you know. If you rush her, she may snap at you. So just be patient!

Happy families

A female dog is call a "bitch." When it is ready to have puppies it is said to be "in heat." Some people have their pets "neutered" or "spayed," which means that they can't have puppies. The reason for this is that it may be hard to find good homes for the puppies. However, if your pet does have puppies, like this mixed breed, she will need extra food and somewhere safe for her family.

Puppy development

In the first eight weeks of life, puppies change from tiny, helpless creatures with closed eyes to fat, squirmy little bundles already showing their individual personalities. After six weeks, most are ready to leave their mothers.

One week old:
eyes still closed,
sleeps a lot

Playing with young puppies

Once the puppies are walking well and the mother dog doesn't mind them being handled, it is very good for the puppies to play with people. It gives them some practice being around people. They find out that people are fun to be with, and they are more likely to become good pets. Always handle puppies gently, and stop playing with them before they get too tired.

Six weeks old: active and curious; starting to eat some solid food

Three weeks old: can focus its eyes and move around

Four months old: full of fun and eager to explore its world

Training your dog

Dogs like food very much, so you can teach your pet new things by giving it a treat each time it does what you want. When you measure out its dry food for the day, take some out to use as rewards. That way it won't be getting a lot of extra food—you don't want it to get too fat. Keep the lessons short but repeat them often until your dog gets the idea.

Teaching your dog "Come"

Your dog will soon learn its name if you look directly at it, call it by name, and say "Come." You can signal by patting your leg at the same time. Give your dog a treat right away but also praise it in an excited voice. Train your pet when it is a little bit hungry. It won't be interested in working for a treat if its belly is full and it feels like sleeping. This Staffordshire Bull Terrier puppy is alert and ready to learn.

Teaching your dog "Heel"

It's no fun going for walks if your dog pulls you down the street or wanders behind you. This Shiba Inu has learned to walk by its owner's side. To teach your dog, start with it sitting on your left side. Hold the leash in your right hand, give it a gentle tug, say "Heel," and take a few steps forward. When your dog begins to walk alongside you, give it a treat and make a fuss of it. Repeat this lesson a few times each day. Increase the length of the "walk" slowly. Your dog will soon be walking beside you on the leash, without pulling.

Teaching your dog "Sit"

1 Start with your pet standing. Holding the treat so that he (or she) can smell it but not get it, move your hand up just above his head and then back toward his tail until he has to bend his back legs.

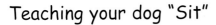 It's a good idea...

...to reward your dog for doing the right thing. Never punish it for making mistakes.

2 As his head follows your hand, his bottom will move down and he will start to crouch. As he sits, say "Sit" clearly and give him the treat. Praise him and make a big fuss to let him know you are pleased with him.

3 Repeat this lesson often, but not for too long at a time. As your dog gets to know what you want when you say "Sit," try starting the exercise with him beside you, or a short distance away from you. Make sure he stays sitting while he eats the treat.

Teaching your dog "Down"

1 Once your pet will sit on command, you can teach her (or him) to lie down. Start with her sitting, then hold the treat right under her nose and move it slowly down to the ground. As she tries to get it, her head will get lower and she will have to lie down. If she stands up instead, don't let her get the treat. Just start again, patiently, with her in the sitting position.

It's a good idea...

...to give commands in a cheerful, happy but firm voice. Never speak angrily to your dog.

2 As she lies down, give a hand signal by pointing to the ground, and say "Down." Give her the treat and praise her right away. When she gets to know what you want, after a bit more practice, try starting the exercise with her beside you, and then a short distance away from you.

Teaching your dog "Stay"

1 Put a long leash on your pet for this lesson so he (or she) can't run away. Start with him sitting down. Stand very still beside him and say "Stay." If he starts to move or goes to lie down, say "Sit" and lead him back into position. Start by keeping him still for just ten seconds, but gradually make him sit still for a little longer each time as he gets the idea. Always give him a treat and lots of praise when he does well.

2 When your pet can stay still with you beside him for a few minutes at a time, slowly get him used to you standing farther away. Hold up your hand in a stay signal as you say "Stay."

3 The last step is for him to get used to you moving away while he remains in the stay position. As you move in front of him, hold up your hand in the stay signal each time you tell him "Stay."

Teaching your dog to do tricks

Because you and your dog are having fun together, training it to do some tricks is a good way to become really good friends. And the more things your dog learns, the better it will become at guessing what you want it to do. Your pet will enjoy all the praise and attention it gets, too.

Make it fun

This Dalmatian loves being the center of attention. Never try to teach your dog anything when it's tired or grumpy. The dog should always enjoy the training sessions. Keep them short, no more than three minutes at a time, but repeat them lots of times through the day.

It's a guessing game

Your dog can't understand words, so it has to guess what you want it to do. The idea is to help your pet to do the behavior "by accident" and then reward it. If it is praised and rewarded each time it does something, it will soon realize that this behavior is what you want.

Teaching "Shake hands"

1 Start with your dog sitting down. Hold the treat hidden in your closed right hand, but let her (or him) smell it. Hold the closed hand, palm side up, in front of her. You can touch her leg lightly with the other hand to help her get the idea of lifting it. Reward her as soon as she begins to lift one paw to try and open your hand.

2 As soon as she lifts her paw a little, take it in your right hand, say "Shake hands," and gently shake her paw. Quickly give the reward and praise her excitedly. Hold your hand a bit higher each time until she is raising her paw to meet your hand. Once she has the idea, only give her the reward when she offers you her paw quickly on command.

Teaching "Roll over"

1 This is an important trick to teach your dog, because it helps him (or her) to understand that you are his leader. Start with your dog lying down. Kneel in front of him with a food treat held firmly in your hand. Reach across behind his head so that he has to turn his head as his nose follows the smell of the treat.

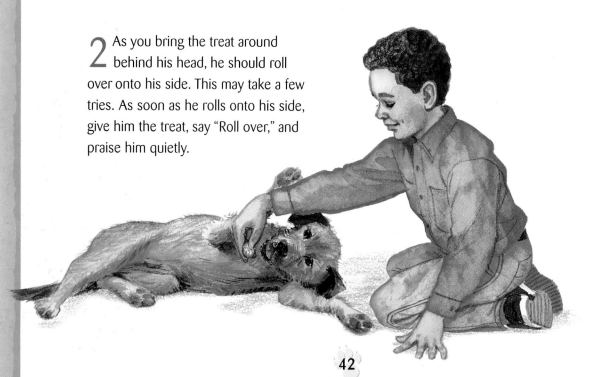

2 As you bring the treat around behind his head, he should roll over onto his side. This may take a few tries. As soon as he rolls onto his side, give him the treat, say "Roll over," and praise him quietly.

3 He may feel anxious when he's in this position. Reassure him by praising him in a quiet voice and encourage him to stay still by stroking his chest gently.

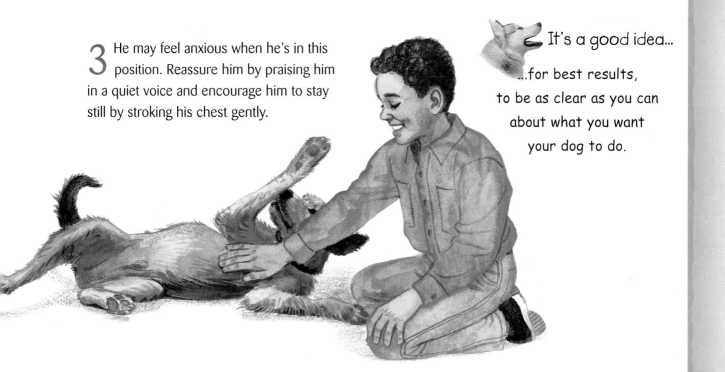

It's a good idea...

...for best results, to be as clear as you can about what you want your dog to do.

4 After he has been practicing for a few days and has the idea of rolling onto his side, take the treat around more behind his neck. Don't give it to him until he has rolled right over onto his back. Then quickly give him the treat, say "Roll over," and quietly praise him some more. Keep him calm by gently stroking his chest and talking softly to him.

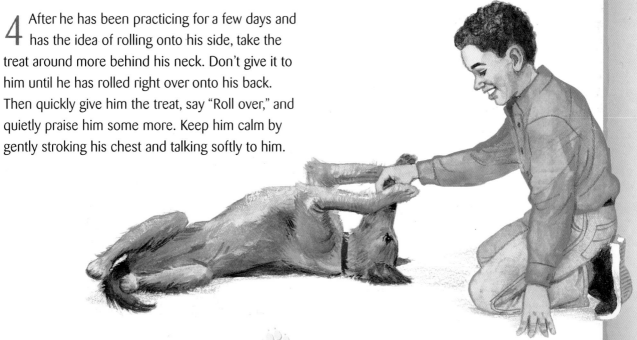

Why does my dog do the things it does?

Dogs (and people) give signals with their bodies that are in a kind of special code called "body language." For example, if you turn off the sound on the TV, you can still tell a lot about what is going on by how the people behave. Watch the things your dog does closely and you will soon begin to understand more. Here are a few examples to help you learn your dog's body language.

Chews up shoes

Dogs like to chew on things. Sometimes they chew on furniture and shoes (like this Boxer is doing) because they are bored or want to play. Shoes smell of the people dogs love, and this makes them happy, especially if they're on their own. To keep your dog out of trouble, be sure it has chew toys of its own instead—and put your shoes away!

Shakes itself after a bath

If a dog is wet, like this Golden Retriever, what it wants most is to be dry. So it shakes to get rid of the water, rushes about madly, and rolls on the grass until it feels comfortable again. If you don't want to be soaked, get out of the way.

Licks my face

This is the way puppies, like this Golden Retriever, greet older or bigger dogs. It's just their way of saying hello and that they're pleased to see you. Because dogs' mouths carry germs, you should gently push or hold your dog out of reach and say "No." Or you could growl at it like its mother does. A good greeting is to tickle your dog under its chin, instead.

Barks a lot

It's natural for dogs like this Jack Russell Terrier to bark—it's another way that dogs "talk" or warn each other of danger. But the noise might cause a problem with neighbors. When your dog barks just to get your attention, ignore it and wait quietly until it stops before you respond. Don't shout at your dog, because it may think you're barking back.

Sniffs everything on walks

A dog's sense of smell is far better than ours. This Golden Retriever will sniff at everything to find out what has been going on in its world. Dogs like to know which other animals have been around recently, their age and sex, and other things about them that dogs find really interesting.

Chases cats

While a dog and cat that live together usually get along perfectly well, most dogs will prick up their ears if a strange cat enters their territory. And if the cat runs away, dogs such as this Kelpie mix just can't help themselves—their natural instinct is to chase it.

Takes a bow

Dogs sometimes "play bow," as this Whippet mix is doing. They bark excitedly and wag their tails. They are saying "Come and play with me." They do this to other dogs and to people. Don't be scared by this kind of barking—the dog is just inviting you to have some fun.

Drools

Like most dogs, this Golden Retriever only drools when it smells food, or when it gets excited, or when it is concentrating on watching something. But breeds like Basset Hounds and Bulldogs drool more than others because their lips can't hold the saliva in their mouths.

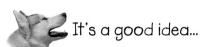

It's a good idea...

...to remember that male dogs usually fight with other males; females fight with other females.

Growls at visitors

Dogs have a strong instinct to defend their territory, so you must think about which places the dog might think belong to it. For example, your dog may not like strangers coming into its yard or too close when it is in a car. So it growls, and may want to bite. After your dog finds out that this is a friend, it will not growl next time. And when you enter a strange dog's territory, be extra careful so that it doesn't bite you.

Your dog is your friend

Everyone likes to be with their friends. Playing, working, or just hanging out are much more fun with a pal. Your dog will be one of the best friends you could ever hope to have. It will share your quiet times and your busy ones. It will make you laugh, and make you feel loved and needed. Remember, a happy, healthy pet is a great pal. Take good care of your dog and it will take the best care of you.

Index

Shar Pei